T0077925

THE DEAD MALL HORROR

A NOVEL IN 49 POEMS

CHAD HELDER

Order this book online at www.trafford.com
or email orders@trafford.com

Most Trafford titles are also available at major online book retailers.

Print information available on the last page.

ISBN: 978-1-6987-0428-9 (sc)
ISBN: 978-1-6987-0430-2 (hc)
ISBN: 978-1-6987-0429-6 (e)

Trafford rev. 11/13/2020

www.trafford.com
North America & international
toll-free: 844-688-6899 (USA & Canada)
fax: 812 355 4082

Dedication

To the intrepid YouTubers who explore creepy abandoned malls.

Contents

The Voices of the Dead Mall

The dead mall held the darkness within,
all of the ghosts together under its wing.
Intruders have heard the voices
crackle through dead speakers in the ceiling,
moan through the earpiece of a dead payphone,
and whisper horrors of the grave
into newfangled ghost-hunting devices.

Once upon a time, years ago
before the electricity ended,
the mall bustled and thrived and grew,
an anthill with skylights and escalators,
thousands of cars on the black asphalt.
After the mall's abandonment,
the voices echoed alone in the moldy shadows
above the green slime of neglected puddles.

A trickle of trespassers visited:
vandals and scrappers,
YouTubers and paranormal investigators,
nothing like the stream of lost shoppers;
the shoppers abandoned the mall.

Sometimes transient spirits
toured the retail mausoleum
to be near happy memories of Orange Julius
across from the video game arcade
with the sliding mirrored door.

Under Its Wing

The ghosts together
under the dead mall's wing,
behind its black curtain,
the dead mall long past insane with grief
since the electricity ended,
trapped in a cadaver of cavernous spaces
without the pitter-patter of customer foot traffic,
the echoing chatter of a crowded food court,
or the babbling
of the majestic central fountain.

The dead mall hovered and surveyed,
its eye in many more places than
security cameras ever reached;
it floated through the towering promenade
of storefront graves
like the weird underwater flight
of a manta ray
above the bleached skeleton
of a coral reef.

The Central Fountain

Once the flowing, pumping heart of the mall
with acrobatic jets of crystal water
and a never-ending waterfall
into the wishing pool
where shoppers cast their pocket change
in little acts of desire.

Just a desecrated corpse of a fountain,
vandalized for years
since the electricity ended
and the waterfall dried up,
tiles cracked and shattered,
blasphemous names in spray paint,
the coins all pocketed by scavengers.

Instead of bubbles and shiny coins,
the sparkling shards of broken glass
from the shot-out skylights
that let the rain inside;
to an intruder it looked like
the mall wept.

In the empty basin,
the raccoon decomposed,
having perished in childbirth,
its babies trapped forever inside.

Stranger Danger

Do you remember freckle-faced Kyle Kenworth?
He was the one they searched for
in every store, in every dark crawlspace,
his face on the billboard by the interstate,
visible from the mall's main entrance,
his smiling face on every orange flyer
under every windshield wiper
in the vast expanse of the parking lot.

The police dogs sniffed out the shallow grave
in the wooded area beyond the parking lot,
but no sign of the severed head.

The rack where Kyle chained his dirtbike,
without a single tire in its teeth,
rusted behind overgrown bushes
as the dead mall decayed.
Once, the police had to cut the chain
to take Kyle's bike as evidence.

After so many years, the missing head
such a treasured prize,
rumors abounded; some speculated
the head might be
on the mall grounds somewhere,
and Kyle's orthodontic retainer
perhaps still in his mouth.

On the Night of Falling Glass

Equipped with their camping lanterns,
hunting rifles, and protective goggles
from the local shooting range,
the motley crew of vandals
set out to rape the dead mall,
a security guard among them,
so they could run amok without fear,
the mall unguarded and betrayed.

The mall had ornate multifaceted skylights
above the central fountain,
above the toddler play area where
they erected Santa's throne at Xmas,
and above the escalators and glass elevator
next to the food court.

From across the empty parking lot,
it sounded like a fireworks display.

After their ammunition spent,
bits of glass
in the rims of their cowboy hats
and crunching beneath their boots,
their adrenaline like lightning,
the pack of vandals savored the mayhem
and left behind
the hollow corpse of the mall
like a victim in a ditch,

the echoing gunshots
followed by moans of grief
and howls for vengeance
as the vandals fled.

The bats gained entrance,
and the waters fell through the gaping
wounds with jagged shards;
the elaborate framework
of the murdered skylights
just a skeleton.

The Treasure in the Floor

Hidden by a carpeted panel in the floor,
the safe once used for the store's nightly deposits
now held the vampire's treasure.

He had many nests in the dead mall,
but this was the vampire's favorite,
the store manager's boxed-in drywall refuge
from the hectic sales floor.
The vampire moved the green metal desk
still full of stationery and empty whiskey bottles,
the desk a shell to protect the treasure
and the vampire's daily undead slumber
as he curled up like a mollusk.

He built a crude lean-to
with shoe department shelving
and a large plastic sheet of green grass
from the massive Easter display,
which formed a snug little cave beneath
like a child playing fort.

He positioned a mannequin in the entryway,
a scarecrow as sentry.

Under the desk with him,
the vampire kept a bearded animatronic elf
who held a little mallet from Santa's workshop.
He named the elf Friend.
He gave the elf all of the details
of his nights alone in the haunted mall
as he snuggled above his treasure in the floor.

The Sliding Mirrored Door

Kyle Kenworth activated the motion sensor
and the sliding mirrored door unveiled
the weird shadowy world
of the arcade,
a dark corridor with flashing games
and spotlighted machines to exchange
dollar bills for tokens
(the police found a token in his pocket).

Crossing the arcade threshold
like stepping into a submarine
of electronic sounds:
the death ribbit of a frog in the street,
chomping dots in the labyrinth of malevolent ghosts,
alien projectiles and hypergalactic acceleration
into the cosmic tempest.

Such concentration upon the screens
to maximize chintzy tokens
adorned with lightning bolts,
no one noticed
the security guard with his eyes upon
tight denim and running shorts
or the presence of a great white shark
scouting just inches away.

The Security Guard

Once upon a time
a moon-faced security guard named Padgett
patrolled the labyrinth of the young mall:
the arcade behind the sliding mirrored door;
the magic shop with a gallery of grotesque masks
where boys shoplifted fake vomit;
the department store
where mannequin doppelgangers
of the all-American nuclear family
witnessed the streaming hordes of shoppers,
where unspeakable assaults occurred
in the claustrophobic cubbies
of locked changing rooms;
the dark forest of the vast parking lot
where an ankle-slasher terrorized salesgirls
at closing time
and a serial killer lured little Hansels and Gretels
into the four-wheeled gingerbread house
of his recreational vehicle.

Padgett was even the backup Santa at Xmas time,
listening to the children's wholesome wishes,
unnerved by the turning animatronic elves.

So much for young Padgett to observe,
smoking cigarettes on break at the back dumpster
by the loading dock,
wandering the parking lot with his flashlight
to catch the ankle-slasher.
When a beautiful man in a peacoat
tempted the security guard into a party van
for a bong hit and a quick rendezvous,
Padgett found himself bitten and sucked dry
by a vampire.

Kyle Kenworth's Day at the Mall

Once, a few weeks after Kyle first heard
AIDS on the radio news,
he rode his dirtbike to the mall
to spend his birthday money,
which he kept in a velcro wallet
in the front pocket of his red powder jacket.
He was eleven.

The friend he telephoned didn't show,
so he wandered the mall alone:
he looked at the broken heart pendants,
which they could engrave at Things Remembered;
perhaps he might give half to a girl
someday.
Kyle watched a boy get his ear pierced
at the fashion accessories store;
the quick thunk of the gun
and the gold stud in the boy's bright red earlobe,
the boy's mother at his side;
Kyle wondered if his father would allow this.
He purchased some sunglasses from the kiosk,
but then worried the tiny screw in the joint
needed tightening.
He scanned the horror covers in Waldenbooks,
not bold enough to buy one.
He threw coins in the fountain
with the muzak mewling overhead.

He played *Frogger* and *Pac-Man* and *Tempest,*
a few tokens left in his pocket.
Torn between the record album or cassette
for Twisted Sister's *Stay Hungry,*
he went with the cassette, easier to conceal.
For lunch he got a large Orange Julius
and a hot dog.

Mang the Mangler

After the skylight massacre,
the dead mall long past hope
of renovation or resurrection,
a corrupt security guard organized
a dog fight,
the toddler play area the perfect pit
beneath the shot-out skylights,
the site of Santa's village at Xmas,
the dogs a mix of everything aggressive
that evil men with prods and chains
can amplify:
English Mastiff
Cane Corso
Rottweiler
Bull Terrier
Gull Dong

The horror of the dog fight:
puddles of blood in the moldy carpeting,
two dozen men shouting,
the aggression a thunderstorm,
snarls of execration and
squeals of agony,
gashes jagged and deep;
money changed hands.

It only happened once,
the police tipped off,
the location too risky afterwards,
but the dead mall remembered;
two dogs perished in the pit,
and victorious Mang the Mangler
died from his wounds on the way home.

The Serial Killer Returns to the Mall

A few months after they found
the headless body of Kyle Kenworth,
the serial killer returned to the mall,
his shabby RV on the western edge
of the vast parking lot.

When Padgett the vampire awoke at sundown,
his nest deep in the mall ductwork,
he sensed the evil in the killer's bloodstream.
Disguised as a shadow,
the vampire crossed the parking lot,
smelling the history of the blood
from many secret crime scenes
inside the killer's RV,
layers of scent too subtle
even for police dogs.

At closing time,
without a fish on the hook,
the serial killer returned to the RV,
finding an unnatural darkness inside,
as black as a mineshaft;
he stepped into the vampire's trap.

Drinking the Serial Killer's Blood

Drinking the serial killer's blood
gave the vampire a jolt of evil,
electrified his black magic,
which was stored in the vampire's reservoir
much like the ink sac of a squid;
the serial killer's blood so full of evil,
the vampire could only sample a small portion.

The vampire delivered a telepathic message
deep into the center of the serial killer's psyche,
planted nightmares of
towering totemic figures
with many monstrous faces
all speaking the same warning message:
stay away from the mall forever.

The vampire erased the fang holes
with his black magic tongue,
and the serial killer woke up the next morning
snug under the covers in the RV top bunk
with a large black blank
on the reel of his memory.
He drove his RV-murder-den away
from the mall parking lot, never to return;
he didn't even notice the missing beer cooler
where he kept Kyle Kenworth's head.

Another Ghost

The ghost of Mang the Mangler,
a huge brindle mastiff mix,
returned to the dead mall,
the dog's sense of smell magnified
in the afterlife.
He could smell the bloodstained carpet
where he fought for his life in the pit;
smell the frogs
asleep in their watery lair
at the bottom of the elevator shaft;
smell the black fungus
crawling up the screen
in the flooded movie theater;
he could smell the vampire.

The specter of the black dog,
who ushers all of his kind
to the land of the dead,
brought Mang back to the mall,
perhaps to atone for the competitors
Mang murdered in the pit.

An unrestful spirit,
Mang wandered every wing of the mall,
each larger than cathedrals;
his paws never disturbed the broken glass.
The dead mall welcomed the huge brindle mastiff mix,
just like the graffiti on the drywall:
MANG THE MANGLER RULES THE PIT

The Medium

The TV medium Maggie Split,
now with her own YouTube channel,
set up the Ouija board
on a tarp like a picnic blanket
in the vast empty anchor store,
vandalized walls distant
in the flashlight beams,
fallen ceiling tiles scattered everywhere,
the smashed perfume counter an island
in the darkness.

Two volunteers from Maggie's community ed
ghost-hunting class
set up the camera on a tripod
to record the seance.

Almost seventy, Maggie Split,
the costar of *Mineshaft Phantoms*
for five seasons,
along with her trusted ghost-hunting team
trespassed deep into the earth
to interview
the crushed, exploded, and suffocated ghosts
from mining catastrophes across the globe.

She wore an eyepatch;
during the third season,
deep in the labyrinth of a copper mine,
an evil spirit blew in her eyeball.

She believed, with enough study and practice,
anyone could become a medium
and speak with the dead;
armed with the best questions,
anyone can interrogate the darkness.

The demolition announced,
the mall abandoned for a decade
since the electricity ended.
It was Maggie's last chance to ask the dead mall
all of her unanswered questions.

The Santa Claus Horror

Just as the early winter darkness
veiled the vast mall parking lot
jam-packed with Xmas traffic,
old chubby Harold pulled on the red pants
of the Santa suit for his evening shift
when a cloud of shadow invaded
the changing room,
and a ceiling tile hit the floor.
With his vampire black magic,
the vampire put Harold in a blackout slumber.

Once, when Padgett was human,
a security guard for the mall,
he filled in
when the Santa called in sick,
his moon face perfect
for the white beard;
the vampire knew the routine.

One by one,
the children marched up the steps
to the ornate Xmas throne
and sat on Santa's lap,
but before they whispered
their list of toys,
the vampire sucked just a mouthful
from their tender necks,
pulling back the winter scarves
adorned with snowmen or reindeer;
not too much blood, even though
nothing tasted better.

He put black spots in their memory
and sealed the fang holes with his tongue.
Not a single shopper could see
Santa's beard saturated with gore
by the end of the evening
or the demonic light in the vampire's eyes
that grew brighter with every mouthful.

None of the children carried a memory,
and they would be untroubled by nightmares,
but every child,
no matter how elderly they became in life
would one day rise from their grave
as a child of Padgett the vampire.
They all carried the vampire's seed,
dormant in their mortal bloodstream,
and Padgett's undead children
would one day multiply,
long after the vampire's obliteration.

Three Occultists on Skateboards

At the witching hour,
three occultists on skateboards
performed the unholy ritual
beneath the empty skylights,
the same spot as the dogfight carnage
and where Santa once sat on his throne.

In their ratty sneakers,
they did the prescribed steps
on top of old dog blood and skylight shards;
they spoke the right ancient words
from the right book bound in skin,
and they opened a portal.

As they packed their
Halloween-store "evil monk" cloaks
into school backpacks,
they thought the ritual failed.

But as they rode through the black mall,
their flashlights guiding them,
passing through patches of skylight moonbeams,
the old skateboard shop filled up
with blinding fluorescence;
all the old merchandise appeared inside:
a retail rainbow of decks, trucks, wheels,
and racks of decals adorned with demon faces.

In disbelief,
the three occultists stood before the portal,
which appeared in a skate shop disguise
much like a candy house
veils a cannibal den.
Welcome boys, said the store manager
with his sharp widow's peak
and eyebrows that met in the center.

The Portal

The invisible portal split open,
offering free passage
from the dark dungeon labyrinth beneath,
from which many ghastly phantoms
yearned to escape,
the old retail shell of the skateboard shop
like the mouth of a tunnel,
the dead mall an open house
for spectral bottom dwellers
shopping for a new home:
a poltergeist with a love for
smashing mirrors,
a banshee with an ear
for empty mall acoustics,
and something old and inhuman
hunting for a new form.
It heard the singing of the frogs
in the flooded elevator shaft
and fell in love.

And only those the dead mall welcomed
could stay,
and the dead mall only welcomed
those willing to cozy up behind
the mall's black curtain
like bat pups suckling
under the protective wing of mother.

More than anything,
the dead mall wanted its human shoppers to return;
it didn't know better.
The dead mall never fathomed demolition.

The YouTuber and the Animatronic Elves

For nostalgia and lost Xmas joy,
the YouTuber filmed an exploration
into the dark dead mall
on a freezing December afternoon
when the mall should have been
overflowing.

Back by the loading dock,
he chose the metal door propped open,
the one with the spray-painted message:
YOU WILL DIE,
the favorite way in for most trespassers.

Many YouTubers have said,
never explore the dead mall alone.

The dead mall felt the YouTuber's love for Xmas;
the dead mall could see into his mind:
many snapshot memories
of Santa's village and the fake snow displays
with the animatronic elves.
The dead mall wanted all of its shoppers
to be happy,
so the animatronic elves came out to play.

As the YouTuber remembered
the bearded elf with the mallet,
he thought he saw one
peeking out from the door
of the smashed-glass elevator;
he noticed little footprints

in the snow on the escalator steps,
the shot-out skylights above;
he heard the jingle of little bells;
he captured one on the camera
as it waved from the vandalized fountain.
He could see its breath in the cold.

The dead mall was happy to play.

As the YouTuber fled the mall,
he heard phantom Xmas muzak,
the speakers hidden everywhere.

He knew he would get millions of views
when he posted the footage on YouTube,
but he watched the playback in horror,
the elves only ever in his mind.

The Inhuman Spirit that Came Through the Portal

It knew
it wanted to be something again;
it inspected the labyrinth of back office corridors
strewn with a chaos of papers,
the empty movie multiplex
home to the black mold,
the food court near the ruined escalator,
and the elevator shaft where the chorus frogs lived.

Many YouTubers and vandals
heard the eerie synchronized calls
echo throughout the dead mall;
the frogs went silent at the sound
of boots on broken glass.
No one could get close.

After the fall of the skylights,
rain and snow invaded the mall,
the water collecting in the elevator shaft;
how the frogs found their way in,
a mystery.

Enchanted by the croaking chorus,
the thing settled down with them
in their cold watery lair.
It froze with them in the winter,
dormant on the edge of death,
listened to their songs and felt
their slimy acts.

It too had known long hibernation
and the pain of metamorphosis.
It felt the tadpoles wiggle and grow.

Ouija Board

At twilight,
a few brown bat stragglers
flew up through the shot-out skylights
to hunt mosquitoes in the night,
their colony in the ceiling above Radio Shack.
The ghost-hunting team prepared the seance,
sweeping away bits of glass,
laying down the tarp,
placing candles on tiers of the fountain,
and positioning the camera
for the YouTube livestream.

Maggie the medium set up the talking board,
removed the patch
from her ghastly white eyeball,
which gave her a pinprick view
through the veil,
and three members of her team
joined her on the tarp,
leaning forward cross-legged
to touch the planchette.

"Is anyone here with us tonight?"

YES

"Can you tell us your name?"

T-I-M-M-Y

Just as the call of the chorus frogs
echoed from across the mall,
the Ouija board spelled:
D-E-M-O-N-F-R-O-G

“Timmy, can you tell me if Kyle Kenworth is still in the mall?”

S-A-F-E

The Last Halloween of the Dead Mall

The graffiti artist, halfway finished
with her mural of the chorus frogs,
left the mall with the bats at twilight,
too dangerous alone at night.

On the mall's last Halloween
before demolition,
many peculiar phantasms
came through the skateshop portal,
which banged open and closed
like shutters in a gale,
some intruders benign
and some parasitic,
as rank as rotten meat.

The vampire, a security guard
so long ago, his memory of it
just shards;
disguised as a shadow,
he watched another livestream seance
by the ruined fountain,
the vampire's belly full
after drinking from a vandal
who slipped on a greenish puddle
by the sweet shop once famous
for caramel apples.

Timmy the Demon Frog
peeked out from its home
in the flooded elevator shaft.

The ghost of Mang the Mangler
trotted along after Kyle Kenworth
who paced around and around
like the shambling mall walkers at dawn;
the apparition of the boy,
lost so long, still looking
for where he chained his dirtbike,
gripping his severed head by the hair,
holding it before him like a lantern
in the Halloween darkness.

What the Vampire Really Looked Like

When he showed himself,
a warm moonlike face,
fuzzy brown sideburns
and pearly whites,
the crisp security guard uniform
with black boots just polished.

What he really looked like:
filthy tattered uniform beneath
the Santa Claus coat
from his night as the jolly old elf;
wild shoots of hair from his ears
and covering his palms;
long black beard
matted with blood,
or sometimes yellowish white hair
after suffering long stretches
of blood abstinence, never by choice;
fangs as brown as tree bark
and sharp as rose thorns;
long fingernail claws, stronger
than rhinoceros horn;
eye contact could mean death.

Tara the Graffiti Artist and the Mural of Frogs

Tara went scouting for the next mural,
riding her dirtbike
alone in the dead mall,
found an empty stretch of drywall
that blocked a bookstore's grave.

Then she heard the call of the chorus frogs
echo through the mall,
but they stopped before she found them;
she rode everywhere looking.

That night,
she walked the mall in her dreams,
a monstrous brindle mastiff beside her;
a friendly man-sized frog waved to her
from the glass elevator. Going down?
It held the door.

The next day,
in her red hoodie, backpack clanking
full of spray paint cans,
she returned to the dead mall,
set up her boombox,
and the mural began.

At first, a psychedelic trio of frogs
was the plan, perhaps a family
with bold black stripes,
brilliant exotic eyes,
and skin shades of greens and browns,

but the mural evolved,
the frog faces became stacked;
three totem poles emerged,
strange ancient frog faces channeled
from somewhere;
by the end she knew the faces,
all ceremonial masks,
a set of demigods from a frog cult
as dead as the mall;
she felt sick making it, at first,
but returned for three days.
She finished it.

She wanted to invite her friends
for beers and celebration at the mural,
but knew she couldn't tell them;
Tara didn't even sign it.
It was only for the dead mall.
It was only for Timmy.

What Blood Can Do

All of the railings
long ago torn out by scrappers,
the drunken vandal stood on the edge
across the courtyard
from the frozen escalators;
bladder bursting,
he pissed a long stream
to the tiled floor below.

Timmy the Demon Frog arose
from its home in the flooded elevator shaft,
gave the fool a push, not even very hard.

Down below,
the ruptured head spilled a puddle
right next to the puddle of urine,
the two not commingling.

The ghost of Mang the Mangler
smelled the blood and urine,
gathered up a kernel of strength
to be just substantial enough
for three laps of his tongue;
something about a canine ghost
and human blood not too dead
that opened a conduit
for a good dose of black magic,
just like a plug in the socket.

And the ghost of Mang the Mangler
became something more,
something larger, eyes lit up
with demonic fire,
something with sharper teeth.

The Drone Flight and the Little Brown Bat

Standing on the tiles of the ruined fountain,
Millicent worked the drone controls,
the contraption not much bigger
than a frisbee.
Her best friend Leakey
linked the footage to the livestream.

The drone zipped through the food court,
hovered high above the escalators,
made a full circuit of the dead mall.
Close to the shot-out skylights,
it flew above the toddler play area
enclosed by planters overgrown
with rain-fed weeds.

Then it plummeted and crashed
to the mossy carpeting below.

Leakey stayed by the gear
as Millicent ran across the mall.
She looked down in horror:
drone smashed beyond hope
and a dead little brown bat,
its wing torn and neck broken,
on its way home
to the colony above Radio Shack
when it collided with the drone.

The dead mall loved its colony of bats.

Both Millicent and Leakey heard

undead Mang awaken,
his barking magnified
by black magic forces.

Millicent and Leakey never seen again,
YouTube detectives studied
every second of the livestreamed footage,
finding three uncanny faces
peeking out from shattered storefronts,
one of them perhaps a frog mask,
another what appeared to be
a bearded face with a Santa hat,
and some speculated
the third an apparition
of freckle-faced Kyle Kenworth.

The Vampire's Mausoleum

The vampire still felt responsible
for mall security,
so he gathered up the bodies,
created a makeshift mausoleum
in the flooded movie theater,
all of the seats torn out,
the waist-high water collecting
downhill by the moldy screen.

The vampire weighted down the bodies
with spare floor tiles from maintenance,
wrapped them up with
an industrial roll of plastic sheeting
and sunk them in the filthy floodwater.

With a can of spray paint,
the vampire wrote
DESECRATORS
across the movie screen, referring to
the chewed-up YouTubers
who murdered a bat with their drone,
the drunk with the crushed head
pushed off the second floor,
and the desiccated mummies
of three skateboarding occultists
sucked dry by demons.

When they finally found the bodies
during the demolition,
the newspaper headline read:
DEAD MALL HORROR

The Wall of Monitors

At the midnight bonfire,
beer cans and cigarette butts
littered everywhere,
Dirk suggested they go explore
the old dead mall.
Nicky said good idea;
it wasn't.

The four of them,
Dirk, Nicky, Andrea, and Spitter,
armed with flashlights,
entered the door with
YOU WILL DIE
in spray paint.

They toured the old food court,
walked up the escalator,
crunchy glass beneath their feet.
Andrea thought she heard the tinkle
of Xmas muzak.
Nicky saw bats,
the moon above the skylights.
Dirk heard taunting little bells.
Spitter saw bloody paw prints by the fountain.

Dirk led the gang down a back hallway
to the security offices where
they found the surveillance room with
the wall of monitors.
A hammer-swinging vandal
smashed them all long ago,

ending up in the ER with
a shard in his eyeball.

Andrea imagined how it looked once:
every monitor another view of the mall,
eyes everywhere.

Spitter screamed when all the monitors
filled with phantom light;
images of the past appeared:
all the cars in the lot,
all the shoppers and their bags,
but the images changed:
every shopper that ever walked there,
mounds of chopped-up bodies,
the fountain geysers of blood,
a spectral illusion born from
the dead mall's anger and despair
at its abandonment.
In the central monitor: the faces of
Dirk, Nicky, Andrea, and Spitter,
their heads on pikes,
a warning to the desecrators.

The Vampire Dreams of Being Human

As Padgett the security guard,
when still counted among mammals,
he had sweat in his armpits
and saliva on his tongue,
back before he slept in crevices,
before the terrible dry throat
of vampire thirst,
before his temperature would drop
to almost frozen solid
like a frog hibernating in a creekbed;
his skin cracked like a mummy,
only softened by feasts of blood.
After he got drained in the back of a van,
his physiology followed
the rules of vampire black magic,
not the biology of living things.

His daydream of being human again:
washing his clothes at the laundromat,
drinking black coffee.
He imagined his interview
on the evening news,
Padgett the security guard a hero
for turning in the long lost head
of the freckle-faced boy,
what the vampire knew he should do,
perhaps receiving a medal from the mayor
and riding in a sunshine parade.
But he sat with the skull in his foul nest,
played with the dead boy's retainer
that never straightened his buck teeth.

The vampire knew
the ghost still searched the mall for it,
the dead boy never resting until
the missing head returned.

The Ghostly Trebles

Vik and Vikki Treble, fraternal twins,
and their twelve-year-old brother Terence
formed a ghost-hunting gang:
The Ghostly Trebles.

They watched the YouTube livestreams:
their hero superstar Maggie Split
holding seances in the dead mall;
they had to go too.

The trio set out with the following:
top-notch smartphone camera,
Polaroid, extra flashlights,
and the newest model of
the Divinator Device.

Nicknamed the banshee-catcher,
The Divinator detected, recorded, and enhanced phantom voices,
carried with an over-the-shoulder strap for active ghost-hunters.
The operator inserted an analog cassette tape
and hit record.
First, the computer detected phantom activity on the tape,
the digital computer filtering the analog signal
for maximum paranormal sensitivity,
isolating and amplifying unexplained voices
(and a range of auditory paranormal phenomena)
for immediate playback with enhanced digital clarity.
The Divinator included a booklet of helpful questions
to ask the spirit world.

The Ghostly Trebles found the door with
YOU WILL DIE in spray paint.
With a fresh set of batteries in the Divinator,
they went inside the door.

The Divinator Device Handbook

Appendix B:
How to Start a Paranormal Interview

Disclaimer: never use the Divinator Device alone.

Standing in the haunted location,
assume an assertive posture
(but never aggressive);
hold the microphone before you
to invite the ghosts to speak,
an important visual cue;
using a calm tone of voice
(use your diaphragm to project)
ask the questions below
(never taunt, mock, or denigrate
the invisible inhabitants):

Is there anyone here with us?
(here you hold out the microphone,
leaving an ample pause)

My name is (blank) and I'm a special investigator
(never say ghost-hunter;
never pretend to be an exorcist)

Can you share your name with us?
(record the ghost's name in your investigator's notebook;
flee the location if the Divinator Device
plays back growling)

Timmy Finds a New Home

A middle-aged bald man
heard about the imminent demolition,
so he returned to the dead mall
to mourn a boy he once loved.

Both seventeen, they once ditched school after lunch
thirty years ago
to hang out at the booming mall.

He walked past the old Zeezo's
where they once tried on zombie masks
and played with a whoopee cushion on display.

He walked through the cavernous ruin
of the department store
where they once French kissed for three minutes
in an empty changing room.

He walked past the empty dead spaces
where the Orange Julius,
the arcade with the mirrored door,
and the sweet shop once existed.

This had happened long before
boys could hold hands in the mall,
but he imagined they did as he
resurrected the ruins of the mall
in his imagination,
the fountain sparkling again.

Soon after their one afternoon together,
the boy fell off the back of a motorcycle,
the driver another boyfriend who lived;
the boy he loved didn't.

Near the food court, he heard the chorus frogs
in the flooded elevator shaft;
they went silent as he approached.

I wish you could come home with me, he said
into the darkness of the elevator shaft,
knowing the frogs would soon perish
in the demolition.

Timmy the Demon Frog
heard the man's invitation;
the demon knew it had to leave,
so Timmy left behind the chorus frogs it loved;
left behind the mural it loved
and the ancient frog cult that
the demon invented just to scare people;
it left behind the dead mall.

Timmy followed the friendly man home,
settled itself into the basement terrarium
with two fat bullfrogs, Mollie and Constance,
a turtle named Chester, and
a lovely arrangement
of plastic pet-store foliage.

Lucien the Psychic and BOA the Spectral Serpent

Lucien, psychic consultant,
spirit medium,
expert practitioner of talking boards,
unofficial exorcist, and
paranormal investigator extraordinaire,
worked with Maggie Split for a season
on her ghost-hunting show.

Well-known for piercing
the supernatural veil
with melodic invocations
and a resonant speaking voice,
Lucien worked with a mysterious
spectral informant nicknamed BOA;
it appeared to Lucien as
a monstrous black serpent.

Fat, grizzled, wheezing,
buttoned up in a peacoat,
Lucien met Maggie at the mall fountain
at dawn;
he spent all night wandering the mall,
heard the ghostly midnight re-enactment of
Mang's bloody dogfight in the pit;
BOA told him many things,
showed him the old skateboard shop
with the open portal to the underworld.

Lucien carried pages
from a medieval witch's black-magic tome
in a red Trapper Keeper tucked under his arm.
With words from the pages,
Lucien closed the portal.

By the ruined fountain, Lucien informed Maggie
about the vampire infestation,
just too many places for the undead thing
to hide from a hunting party.
BOA told Lucien about the inhuman spirit
pretending to be a frog;
BOA and Lucien both loved the mural.

Maggie asked: What is the dead mall?

Smoking a cigarette,
Lucien translated for BOA: the mall
is a shell, but not dead at all.
Once overflowing with life like
the water in this fountain,
the shoppers now replaced with
spectral denizens,
the dead mall presides over a dark carnival;
there is a primary entity
at the heart of the dead mall,
something ancient and empty;
the dead mall keeps its remaining family
safe and warm behind the veil
like a comforting mother's quilt,
a patchwork phantasmagoria.
The dead mall only pretends to be a mall,
composed of memories and wayward spirits.
Like every psyche, mortal or otherwise,
the bulk of its contents hidden deep

in the black space of unconscious shadow.
The mall has its family:
Timmy the Demon Frog,
Mang the Mangler,
the vampire security guard,
a colony of brown bats,
and the lost beheaded boy

Maggie: Is Kyle Kenworth still here?

Lucien: BOA tells me your son is still here.

Unexplained Phenomena

The Ghostly Trebles,
the sibling ghost-hunting gang,
explored the dead mall,
Vikki carrying the Divinator Device,
Vik taking snapshots with the Polaroid,
little brother Terence following behind.

At the old toddler play area,
the Divinator Device emitted a chime for
anomalous auditory phenomenon detected;
the device played back
spectral baying of Mang the Mangler.

Near the food court,
the chime for phantom voice detected.

Divinator Device: WELCOME

Vik: Wow that's friendly.

Divinator Device: ENJOY SHOPPING

Vikki: The ghost thinks the mall is still open.

Divinator Device: PLEASE NEVER LEAVE ME

Terence: That's not good.

In the corner of his eye,
Terence saw the animatronic Xmas elf
in the planter overgrown with weeds.

After a double take, it vanished.

The specter of a medieval king,
who once made a foul pact with the devil,
escaped from the underworld
when the skateboarders opened the portal.
At the fountain, he circled around the siblings
and whispered into the device.

Divinator Device: BEWARE VAMPIRE

The ghost-hunters saw a security guard approaching
with his crisp beige uniform and shiny boots.
Vik noticed the sun had set.

They ran for their lives across the mall,
through the empty cavernous department store,
down the back hallway,
out the metal door with
YOU WILL DIE in spray paint.
They scrambled into the car.
Vik hit the accelerator;
just as the car reached the edge
of the vast parking lot,
the Divinator Device chimed.

PLEASE COME BACK

Polaroids

When the Ghostly Trebles explored the dead mall,
Vik took a series of photographs with the Polaroid camera.

Polaroid One: The Desecrated Fountain

Above the blasphemous graffiti and cracked tiles,
phantom spurts of water,
as if the fountain daydreamed
about its lost beauty,
and what appears to be
a translucent sheet floating above,
perhaps a cloak
that concealed a midair specter.

Polaroid Two: Ghostly Hand

In the only changing room
with a mirror intact,
a child's fingers
peeking out from the stall door,
but no feet visible beneath,
the mirror revealing
an empty changing room.
The fingers might have blue nail polish.

Polaroid Three: Balls of Static

Descending the escalator,
three balls of brown static,
two the size of a basketball,
the third somewhat smaller,

each with three yellow glowing eyes,
perhaps a family of demonic entities
on their last tour of the mall.

Polaroid Four: Weed Face

In a tangled mass of overgrown weeds
in the planter beneath the shot-out skylights,
the jagged leaves seem to make up
a face in torment,
the eyes mournful holes of shadow.

The Ankle-Slasher

After a long shift making caramel apples,
the babbling fountain just outside the sweet shop
lulling her into daydreams,
Jill put on her red puffy ski jacket,
her golden feathered hair
parted down the middle.
She pulled down the security gate,
saying goodnight to various retail clerks
passing by.

Out in the freezing dark parking lot,
her car parked on the outer edge
where the streetlights barely reached,
feeling very alone all of a sudden,
she quickened her pace,
careful not to slip on shiny ice patches.

Car keys ready, she got inside,
started up the reluctant engine,
but still had to scrape the windshield.
Wishing she had brought her gloves,
she started scraping,
noticing the orange flyer
stuck underneath
frozen windshield wipers.

When the warm air from the dashboard vent
finally loosed the wipers,
she tried to read the smeared flyer:
MALL PATRONS AND STAFF BEWARE

The ankle-slasher struck from beneath the car
like a trap door spider,
slashing at her Achilles tendons
with the straight razor.
She hit the icy asphalt.
Like a spider immobilizes a hapless grasshopper
in sticky silk,
the ankle-slasher bound her with duct tape.

The car nice and warm,
the windshield clear of ice,
he drove away with Jill in the trunk.

Every time the ankle-slasher returned to the mall,
he purchased a caramel apple from the sweet shop,
enjoying it on the bench
by the babbling fountain
in memory of Jill,
savoring what he had done to her,
a straight razor in his pocket.

The Ankle-Slasher Returns

An old man, the ankle-slasher
dreamed of the mall in his prison bunk,
relishing the obscene atrocities
of the serial killer game,
when a massive stroke plucked him
from the world of the living.

Wandering the dead mall,
still in his prison jumpsuit,
the ghost visited the ruined fountain
and the retail grave of the sweet shop,
the old display counters once filled
with delicious caramel apples,
now smashed and empty.

The vampire saw the ghost first.
Once a security guard,
his job to protect retail clerks
from parking lot perverts
(in later years just sampling
the mall employees, never draining),
he called upon Mang the Mangler.

Electrified with ancient black magic,
the monstrous brindle mastiff
welcomed the ankle-slasher
by mangling and dismembering
the killer's spectral body,
agony even for a ghost.

Jill the sweet shop clerk,
haunting the mall for over thirty years,
materialized to witness the retribution,
her phantom eschewing legs
for what the ankle-slasher did to her,
just a floating torso,
her hands still bound,
her mouth still covered
with the slasher's duct tape,
her eyes reflecting the horror of her fate.

All thirteen of his parking lot victims
from many different malls,
all legless phantom torsos
joined Jill to watch.

Timmy the Demon Frog
rose up from its home
in the flooded elevator shaft.

Many occult scholars have noted,
if you dig deep into black magic grimoires,
you will find references to inhuman demons
devouring human ghosts.

With one whiplike strike of its frog tongue,
Timmy scooped up the spectral remains
of the ankle-slasher,
swallowed all of his dismembered pieces
and obliterated him forever.

The thirteen phantom victims,
now free of duct tape bindings,
their legs returned,
followed Timmy the Demon Frog;
it ushered them to the next world,
a special realm
with meadows, babbling streams,
and no asphalt parking lots.

The Vampire's Slimy Puddle

Beneath the shot-out skylights,
puddles of rain and melted snow formed,
mall floor tiles slick
with green slime and black mud,
peppered with shards of broken glass.

After sunset, the vampire hid himself
behind the overgrown planters,
peering through the weeds,
stalking a puddle
like a polar bear stalks a hole in the ice
where seals emerge for oxygen;
the vampire waited for trespassers to slip,
twilight optimum hunting time.

Like every fan of vampire movies knows,
a vampire's reflection doesn't appear in a puddle,
but only the most adept vampire scholars know
a vampire can cast hallucinations into a calm puddle
like a ventriloquist throws his voice into a dummy.

Passing by the vampire's puddle,
like a kid crossing the troll's bridge,
your eyes might be distracted
by a flash of light from the murky puddle,
at first perhaps your flashlight beam,
but as you approach, the calm surface
lights up,
reflects back the ghosts of the former mall,
visions of retail splendor, a row of caramel apples
aglow in the warm light of the display cabinet.

Or the vampire might show you
the snapshot of your childhood home,
retrieved from your frontal lobe
with black magic telepathy,
the image so real you think
you could step into it.

Or he might show you
the most popular high school clique
beckoning for you to join them
back in your '80s memories,
all with desire in their eyes.

Or he might show you
a circle of black-clad mourners
around your fresh grave.

Mesmerized by the vision in the puddle,
you become docile;
your first step in motion when
the vampire moves in.

The Vault of Xmas Wonders

Deep in the innards of the dead mall,
a labyrinth of corridors, endless doors,
some broken through
and everything plundered within.
Separated from her band of YouTubers,
Charleigh tried a doorknob; it opened.

Her flashlight revealed
a vault of wonders,
the long lost Xmas storage room.
Like an archaeologist from a '30s horror flick
desecrating the golden splendors
of an undisturbed Egyptian tomb,
Charleigh entered the Xmas storage room
with no thought of curses.

Charleigh had found at last
the legendary Xmas trove
sought after by YouTube explorers.
It was all there, untouched
since the mall's final Xmas,
her footage bound to be
a YouTube sensation.

At the center of the room, Santa's throne,
red with hand-painted holly,
worth a fortune on eBay.
Every Xmas of her childhood,
she sat on Santa's lap,
no matter how long the wait.

A throng of animatronic elves
holding mallets, chisels,
and woodworking saws
to make toys for the children;
Charleigh didn't think of the tools as weapons.

A full-sized reindeer
for children to sit in the saddle
and have their picture taken
like the one in Charleigh's scrapbook.

So many Xmas trees,
some with a frosting of plastic ice,
some with red mirrored balls.

She thought she heard an animatronic elf
move its saw back and forth.
A man in a Santa Claus suit
arose from a crate.

After searching for hours,
her friends found Charleigh at last.
Covered in soot
and the excrement of bats,
she walked in circles around
the empty storage room,
holding out her camera,
the screen black, battery dead,
muttering to herself:
back and forth
back and forth
back and forth

Escalators in the Snow

The intrepid photographer who
captured haunting images of abandoned places:
the theme park based on Grimm's fairy tales
where visitors peek through the cabin window,
the wolf in grandmother's nightgown
under a blanket of cobwebs,
animatronics visible through patches of fur;
the elementary school evacuated
after the nuclear accident,
finger paintings still pinned to the wall;
the My Buddy doll with the punctured head
in the mental hospital
infamous for neglecting children.

The morning after the snowstorm,
the whole mall frozen in silence,
the bat colony cozy in deep hibernation,
six inches of snow on the dead escalators,
fresh and pristine
beneath the shot-out skylights;
he took the photographs that went viral.

Upon closer inspection,
naked footprints on the steps.

During the night,
the vampire descended the escalator;
the snow felt good on hardened soles
used to walking on skylight shards.
Halfway down,
the vampire stopped,
tongue stuck out to catch snowflakes.

The Legend of Kyle Kenworth

In black trenchcoat and slouch hat,
Dolph took his patrons on ghost tours
of the historic district,
the hip restaurant built on the site
where an orphanage burned down,
dishwashing staff haunted by
charred children trailing ashes
that can be plucked from the air.

Sometimes, he found some customers
here and there
willing to pay a little extra
for a midnight tour of the dead mall,
technically trespassing,
so Dolph kept it off the books.

Soon the dead mall would be gone,
wrecking machines gathering
in the vast parking lot.

He parked the passenger van
near the loading dock
and the door with YOU WILL DIE
written in spray paint,
the six German tourists thrilled
at crossing the taboo threshold.

As they promenaded past the retail graves,
Dolph told them the legend of Kyle Kenworth:
abducted from the mall and murdered
over thirty years ago,

the missing head a legendary prize
rumored to be hidden in the mall.
In later years before the electricity ended,
retail clerks sometimes spotted
the disembodied head
bobbing in the fountain
or whispering gibberish
inside the trash compactor. Once,
a store manager saw the head
inside a floor safe. In every case,
mall security found nothing.
Ghost-hunters once claimed
the head floated through the mall,
fluttering bats swirling around.
A squatter saw him by the escalators,
his head attached with an Ace bandage
from the sporting goods store.
Many reports of him standing by the edge
where scrappers stole the railings,
staring down,
wearing the red powder jacket,
spectral head in his hands,
the demonic brindle mastiff beside him.
Ghost-hunters recorded EVPs
again and again:
I can't find my bike. I need to call my mom.

Maggie Split heard the tour group approaching.
She hid behind a pillar in Radio Shack as they passed,
noticing the fallen ceiling tiles
and piles of bat shit.

The Skull

Kyle Kenworth loved the wall of stuffed animals
in the old Hallmark store, even though
the boy thought he should have outgrown them,
something only a mother a would know,
so Maggie set up her Ouija board there
in front of the empty shelving.

In the candlelight,
the planchette spelled out:
C-A-L-L-M-Y-M-O-M

I'm here, she cried out.
Your mom is here, Kyle.

She sensed movement
at the mouth of the retail shell;
she turned around.
Out of the darkness, a security guard
appeared, crisp beige uniform,
shiny black boots.
A moon-faced young man with fuzzy sideburns,
he carried a beer cooler.

I found this, the security guard said.
I think maybe it belongs to you.

Maggie removed the patch
from her strange milky eye
that was only blind to the mortal realm;
she glimpsed the vampire's true appearance.
In a heartbeat he was gone.

She shined a flashlight inside the cooler:
an animatronic elf from the old Xmas displays
and a red velvet bag with a drawstring
containing her son's missing skull and
orthodontic retainer.

A Post-it Note on the inside of the cooler lid:
Give them a good home, it read
in the vampire's messy scrawl.

Agnes the Mall Walker

In her bright yellow jumpsuit,
matching headband, Reeboks,
and white curls,
Agnes an early adopter
of the mall-walking craze;
always safe from muggers,
never icy patches like a sidewalk,
the mall a perfect 70 degrees,
Agnes made endless circuits
through the mall before opening,
diligent with heart rate checks.
Grouchy retail clerks with their morning coffee
nodded hello in passing.

In 1989, Agnes dropped dead
right outside Sears; a security guard
caught it on the monitor,
but CPR too late.

Agnes never left the mall.
Shoppers throwing coins in the fountain
sometimes saw a smiling figure in yellow
beside them in the surface reflection.
A dapper silver gentleman chatted with Agnes
all along the mall's promenade,
only for her to evaporate by the cineplex
before he could get her number.

Long after the electricity ended
and the mall's decay accelerated,
Agnes still walked the mall at dawn,

her short white curls now long iron locks,
bright denture smile never faltering,
just some green patches visible
beneath her yellow headband.
Ghost-hunters captured bright yellow blurs
on their Polaroids,
and her EVPs on the Divinator Device
always welcoming and cheerful.

Lucien the spirit medium
walked a lap with her at dawn.

Lucien: Have you seen a little boy in a red jacket?

Agnes: Oh yes that's Kyle. Such a sweet boy, and his loyal dog Mang. He can't seem to find his bicycle.

Lucien: Do you know the mall will soon be gone?

Agnes: They're always saying that, but it does seem maintenance has declined lately.

Lucien: There's another path you should try.

Lucien's spectral guide BOA, an adept psychopomp,
took the form of a dutiful Eagle Scout,
guided Agnes down a different road,
and Agnes walked herself out of the mall;
she went much farther than ever before.

The Ceremony

At the center of the ruined fountain
beneath the shot-out skylights,
Lucien built a small pyre,
just large enough for a boy's skull.

Maggie set up the candles,
placed the red velvet bag
containing Kyle's skull
and orthodontic retainer
on top of the ceremonial pyre.
Lucien nodded; it was time.

The ghost of Kyle Kenworth
had wandered the mall long enough.

Inside his dilapidated red Trapper Keeper,
Lucien kept some taped-together pages
from the medieval witch's grimoire,
a spell to release a trapped ghost
bound to earthly remains.

So many years ago Maggie lost her boy,
so many years she scoured
the paranormal underbelly,
traveling deep into the earth,
traveling deep into black pockets
of forbidden knowledge.

Lucien called upon BOA, his spectral guide;
appearing as a serpentine shadow,
the inhuman spirit carried the spark of fire
on its tongue,
and it ignited the pyre.

At first the flames lapped up the velvet bag,
orbital sockets revealed inside,
but then the flames turned an unnatural green
with black smoke magnifying the darkness;
the smoke carried voices,
phrases from ancient dead languages,
and demonic eyes peeking through the veil.
In a flash, the pyre gone,
just a black smudge on the vandalized fountain.

Maggie turned on her flashlight,
Kyle Kenworth standing in the beam.

Maggie reached out to the apparition;
Kyle couldn't see her,
lost in a ghost's nightmare.

The Procession

The ceremony complete,
skull destroyed, the tether broken,
Lucien recited more strange phrases
from the tattered page of the grimoire,
and BOA pulled back the veil;
the procession through the dead mall
had begun:

Boys and girls
marching in pairs,
a procession
of ghostly decapitated children,
each cradling their head, face forward,
eyes calm and purposeful,
they sang a simple rhythmic hymn,
mall acoustics carrying the tune
to every dark corner,
each child's mouth an open O
as they sang the wordless song
in unison.

From across history
the child ghosts gathered
to escort Kyle Kenworth,
each with a tale as tragic,
some heads lost in gruesome collisions,
some swept away by cannonballs;
the terrible swipe
of a grizzly bear paw
or a flying pane of glass;
some who encountered a taut wire

across a bike path.
Like Kyle, some ran afoul
of evil men with hatchets,
heads later found
in basement freezers
or pickled in specimen jars;
some beheaded
in sacrifices to vengeful gods.

All victims,
now standing together
in a chain of grief
for the ascension of Kyle Kenworth.

At the end of the grim parade,
a little girl without a partner
held out her hand to Kyle;
he already knew the tune.

Mang trailed behind the procession,
whining as the children vanished
into a spectral mist;
Mang could not follow his boy.

Lucien comforted Maggie
on the bench by the ruined fountain,
pouring a cup of tea from his thermos
as Maggie cried tears of relief,
her murdered son home at last.

Imelda and the Bat Report

Imelda decided to do a bat report
for 8th grade biology class,
so she asked her big brother
to take her exploring in the mall,
her biology teacher unaware.

Her brother took Imelda to the door
with YOU WILL DIE in spray paint,
but the demolition company had locked it.
Imelda noticed an alternative:
a piece of plywood pried loose.

They timed their arrival perfectly;
at the escalators in the twilight,
the colony of bats came rushing in
from their home above the Radio Shack.
The shot-out skylights so high,
and the route to them so direct,
the stream of bats formed a spiral
of wing-fluttering velocity and ascension
to clear the opening above
and search the night for insects.

It was the most beautiful thing
Imelda had ever seen;
her brother agreed.
She realized her bat report
would have to be a poem.

They didn't know it,
but they had witnessed the last night
of the bats, the colony abandoned.
Biologists would have a hard time
explaining it.

The wrecking machines gathering
at the edge of the parking lot,
the dead mall turned its will
upon the dispersal of the bats,
forcing them to find
new roosts for hibernation,
every bat as precious to the dead mall
as every lost shopper.

That night,
after finishing her bat poem,
Imelda dreamed she flew with them
as they found cozy new homes
inside accommodating belfries.

Her bat report received an A.

Death of a Vampire

Even though he murdered some,
cursed many to the nightmare
of vampirism after death,
hid bodies in the flooded theater,
and kept Kyle Kenworth's head
as his secret treasure;
in his mind,
the vampire was always
true to the mall,
a true security guard,
and he couldn't exist elsewhere.

Every fan of horror movies knows,
a vampire is treacherous
and difficult to kill; however,
very few vampire scholars know this secret:
the leading cause of vampire death
is suicide,
the curse of lonely everlasting life.
The laws of vampire black magic
make it quite easy for them.

His treasure given back to the mother,
no more children to sip from at Xmas,
the razing of the dead mall imminent,
the vampire returned to his favorite nest
and snuffed himself out with an ancient spell
that every vampire knows by heart.

Off to the next world,
even Padgett the security guard-turned-vampire
didn't know what that was.

By the time the wrecking machines
reached his nest,
just a mound of vampire ash.

The Razing of the Dead Mall

To excavate, to dig
sounds much like discovery,
to uncover what's buried beneath
like archaeological treasures
or the truth of mass graves,
but the demolition excavator
enacts destruction
with its terrible metal arm,
feet like a war tank,
and hydraulic claw,
a wrecking machine monster
like an unspeakable something
from the bottom of a black lake.

The excavators beset the dead mall
on all sides,
the demolition delayed for a short time
when they found dead bodies
in the flooded movie theater.

The YouTubers came again,
this time with their drones
to watch from above:
the dead mall
like a magnificent sperm whale
murdered beside a ship,
the whalers cutting in from above,
the sharks in a feeding frenzy beneath.

The Spirit of the Dead Mall

The vast new Amazon distribution center
stood; the dead mall didn't,
its bones obliterated,
its ghosts scattered.

Before a shopping mall,
the land once supported
a cattle farm.
Before that, perhaps a forest;
no one seems to remember.

The trucks come and go
from the Amazon distribution center,
as do the workers,
just like those lost shoppers,
now shopping alone
through their screens.

And the spirit of the dead mall,
the thing that took
so many ghostly denizens
under its wing;
BOA the spectral serpent
once said:
the dead mall only pretended
to be a mall.
It descended deep beneath the land,
perhaps to hibernate for a time,
or to incubate,
perhaps to rise again.

The End

From the wooded area
adjacent to the vast parking lot,
Mang the Mangler
watched the Amazon trucks
come and go.

Some afternoons, the brindle mastiff rested
on the site of Kyle's shallow grave
where they found the headless body
so many years ago;
it made Mang feel close to him somehow.

It seemed like years went by.

The specter of the black dog,
who ushers all of his kind
to the land of the dead,
appeared on the horizon again;
time for Mang to go,
his dead mall purgatory
deemed satisfactory.

The black dog's long snout
pointed toward eternity,
the canine psychopomp proceeded;
Mang followed.

Timeline

1978: The shopping mall opens to much local fanfare.

1981: The management company hires Jeremy Padgett as a security guard.

1982: The mall undergoes a massive expansion.

1983: The rapist and serial killer known as "The Ankle-Slasher" abducts a mall employee in the parking lot at closing time.

1984: The abduction of Kyle Kenworth from the mall. After a nationwide search and media campaign to find the missing boy, Kyle's decapitated body is found in a wooded area just beyond the parking lot, buried in a shallow grave. The boy's severed head is never recovered. Padgett the security guard fails to show up for work, his car found in the mall parking lot; he is never seen again.

1988: One of the anchor stores is converted into a cinema multiplex.

1992: The mall reaches its peak capacity of 118 retail stores, 4 anchor stores, and approximately 6,000 parking spaces.

2002: Two of the anchor stores become bargain outlets.

2006: The cinema multiplex closes; the mall occupancy falls to 10 percent.

2007: The mall officially closes and the electricity is shut off.

2008: A gang of vandals shoot out all of the skylights and an illicit dogfight is held in the mall, both facilitated by a corrupt security guard.

2010: The contract with the security company is not renewed; the mall is extensively vandalized and scavenged for scraps.

2012: Three teenage boys, dabbling in the occult, disappear from the abandoned mall.

2015: Now the most infamous abandoned mall in the country, a symbol of a bygone era, the abandoned mall is frequently explored and documented by YouTubers.

2017: Maggie Split, the star of ghost-hunting reality shows, holds a series of seances that are livestreamed on YouTube. An anonymous graffiti artist creates the mysterious frog mural, which is later shared widely on social media. Two YouTubers disappear after recording drone footage of the mall.

2018: Following a complex series of bankruptcies and extended litigation, the demolition of the mall commences. Bodies are discovered in the flooded movie theater. The newspaper headline reads: "Dead Mall Horror." The abandoned mall is razed to the ground.

2020: The vast new Amazon distribution center is erected on the site of the former shopping mall.

Printed in the United States
By Bookmasters